First Facts®

Rain and Life in a Nigerian Village

the BIG PICTURE

CAPSTONE PRESS
a capstone imprint

Catherine Chambers

First Facts is published by Capstone Press, a Capstone imprint,
151 Good Counsel Drive, P.O. Box 669, Mankato, Minnesota 56002.
www.capstonepub.com

First published in 2010 by A&C Black Publishers Limited, 36 Soho Square, London W1D 3QY
www.acblack.com
Copyright © A&C Black Ltd. 2010

Produced for A&C Black by Calcium. www.calciumcreative.co.uk

032010
005746ACF10

Library of Congress Cataloging-in-Publication Data
Chambers, Catherine, 1954-
  Rain and life in a Nigerian village / by Catherine Chambers.
     p. cm. — (First facts, the big picture)
  Includes bibliographical references and index.
  ISBN 978-1-4296-5507-1 (library binding)
  ISBN 978-1-4296-5517-0 (paperback)
  1. Rain and rainfall—Nigeria—Juvenile literature. I. Title. II.
Series.

QC925.6.N6C43 2011
630.9669—dc22   2010012857

Every effort has been made to trace copyright holders and to obtain their permission for use of copyright material.

This book is produced using paper that is made from wood grown in managed, sustainable forests. It is natural,
renewable and recyclable. The logging and manufacturing processes conform to the environmental regulations
of the country of origin.

Acknowledgements

The publishers would like to thank the following for their kind permission to reproduce their photographs:

Cover: Corbis: Gianni Giansanti (front); Fotolia: Maria Adelaide Silva (back). **Pages:** Alamy Images: Wayne
Hutchinson 16, Giles Moberly 18-19; Corbis: Ed Kashi 11, 14-15; Fotolia: Aureleiii 2-3, Denis Cordier 6, Maria
Adelaide Silva 6-7; Shutterstock: Anton Albert 4, Andrew Chin 14-15, Lucian Coman 20-21, Dainis Derics 4-5,
20-21, Fonats 8-9, Gkuna 16-17, JCPJR 10-11, Gregor Kervina 1, Muriel Lasure 3, 12, 12-13, Chris Leachman 17,
Frances A. Miller 22-23, Louie Schoeman 24, Konstantin Sutyagin 9, Tish1 18-19, Yaro 7.

Contents

Rain

We cannot live without rain. It helps our **crops** to grow and gives us water to drink.

Meet Adamu

*"I live in a country called Nigeria, in **Africa**. It is often dry where I live."*

How much?

Some parts of Africa have too much rain. Other parts do not have enough. Very little rain falls in the part of Nigeria where Adamu lives.

Hi!

Find out about rain where I live.

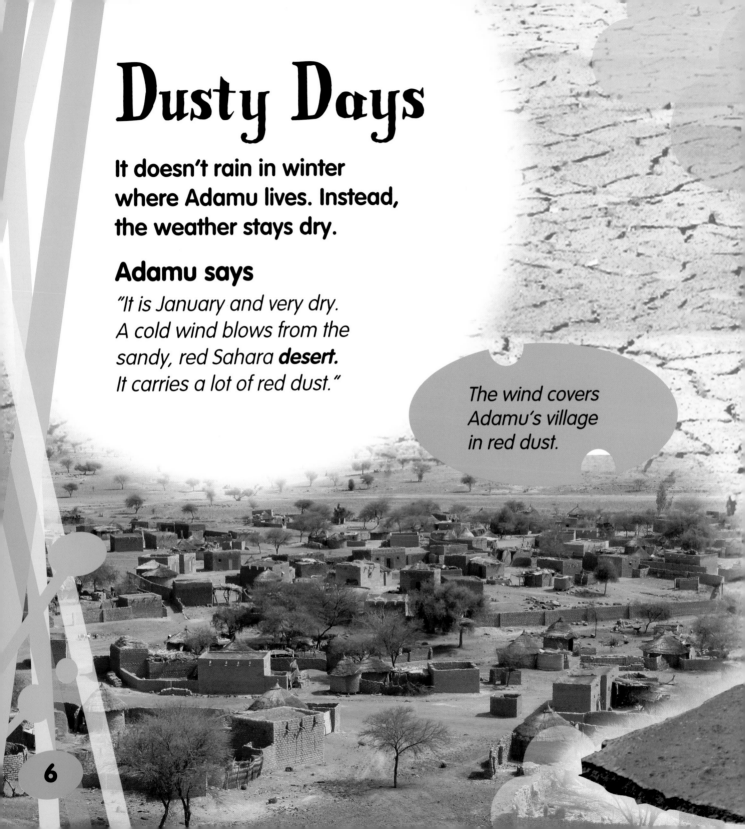

Dusty Days

It doesn't rain in winter where Adamu lives. Instead, the weather stays dry.

Adamu says

*"It is January and very dry. A cold wind blows from the sandy, red Sahara **desert**. It carries a lot of red dust."*

The wind covers Adamu's village in red dust.

6

Dry rivers

By March, the dusty ground is cracking.
Rivers are dry. It is hard for Adamu's family
to water their tomato and pepper crops.

Dry, dry, dry

Will it Rain?

In April, the people in Adamu's village wait for it to rain.

Adamu says

"Now a different wind is blowing dark storm clouds from the ocean to my village. When the clouds get here, it will rain."

A storm is coming

Rain clouds

Rain falls gently from pale gray clouds. When there is a storm, rain pours from dark clouds.

Everyone is waiting for the rain.

9

Rain at Last!

Dark rain clouds race toward Adamu's village. The clouds are heavy and wet. It starts to rain.

Adamu says

"My family loves the rain. The rain will water the dry ground. I think the thunder and lightning are scary! I run inside to hide."

Flash! Bang!

Food to eat

The rain means that Adamu's family can start to grow crops, so they will have food to eat.

Adamu's mother is happy now the rain is here.

11

Time to Farm

It is May. Because of the rain, the earth is red and damp. It is time to start farming!

Adamu says

"My family sows crop **seeds** in long piles of soil. Deep dips between the piles hold the rainwater."

Cattle **plow** the soil so it is ready for the seeds.

We grow...

Adamu's family sows **maize** and **millet** seeds and groundnuts. Groundnuts are tasty peanuts. They grow under the ground.

Wet, wet, wet

Danger!

It is June, and the rain still falls. It fills the rivers. If too much rain falls, the rivers may **flood**.

Adamu says

"My father and I travel to the city to buy more seeds. The rain has fallen so heavily that the roads are flooded."

Heavy rain makes the dirt roads muddy.

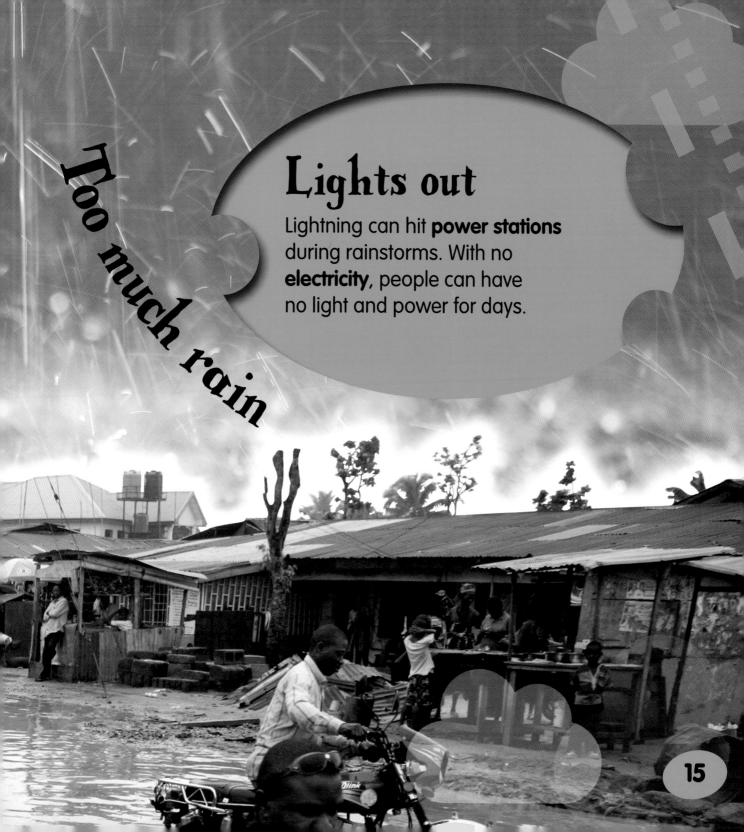

Too much rain

Lights out

Lightning can hit **power stations** during rainstorms. With no **electricity**, people can have no light and power for days.

Drying Out

In September, the rain is light. The land slowly dries out. It is time to sow vegetable seeds.

Adamu says

"My family grows vegetables in a small, wet field near the river. It is called a fadama."

Hoe, hoe, hoe

The soil is dug with a **hoe** before the seeds are planted.

We plant...

Adamu's family plants tomatoes, spinach, **okra**, sweet peppers, and onions in the field. Bananas are sometimes planted too.

No More Rain

It is October. There will be no more rain now until next year. The crops have dried in the sun.

Adamu says

*"It is time to **harvest** the crops. Drummers play music to help everyone work. Harvesttime is fun!"*

Drummers play to celebrate the harvest.

Harvesttime

People in Adamu's village harvest millet and maize crops. The **grain** from the crops can be made into flour for food such as bread and cereal.

Work to the beat!

19

Dry Again

It is December. A dry wind blows from the Sahara again. Everything is covered in red dust once more.

Adamu says

"We do not farm during the winter when there is no rain. This means I can go to school."

Whoosh!

Water to last

Adamu's village has a **well**. The villagers use water from the well during the dry season when there is no rain.

Now Adamu has time for schoolwork—and play!

21

Glossary

Africa large area of land with many countries

crops plants people grow for food

desert hot, dry, dusty or rocky place

electricity power for lights and machines

flood when water breaks out of a river and spreads onto land around the river

grain small seed of a plant

harvest to cut down or pick crops

hoe tool used to dig up soil

maize crop that is made into flour

millet crop that is made into flour

okra long, thin, green vegetable

plow to dig up and turn over soil

power stations places where power such as electricity is made

seeds parts of a plant from which new plants grow

well hole in the ground where water is stored

Further Reading

FactHound offers a safe, fun way to find Internet sites related to this book. All of the sites on FactHound have been researched by our staff.

Here's all you do:

Visit www.facthound.com

FactHound will fetch the best sites for you!

Books

A is for Africa by Ifeoma Onyefulu, Cobblehill Books, (1993).

Drought (Wild Weather) by Catherine Chambers, Heinemann Library (2007).

Looking at Nigeria (Looking at Countries) by Jillian Powell, Gareth Stevens (2007).

Index